A PATH
THROUGH
LOSS

A Guide
to Writing Your
Healing & Growth

ALSO BY NANCY REEVES

I'd Say Yes, God, If I Knew What You Wanted:
Spiritual Discernment

NANCY REEVES PHD

A PATH
THROUGH
LOSS

A guide
to writing your
healing & growth

Northstone

Editor: Michael Schwartzentruber
Cover & interior design: Margaret Kyle
Proofreading: Dianne Greenslade
Cover photo: Copyright ©1999 Bob Brinton. Used with permission.

Northstone Publishing acknowledges the financial support
of the Government of Canada, through the Book Publishing
Industry Development Program, for its publishing activities.

Northstone Publishing is an imprint of Wood Lake Books Inc.,
an employee-owned company, and is committed to caring for the
environment and all creation. Northstone recycles and reuses
and encourages readers to do the same. Resources are printed on recycled
paper and more environmentally friendly groundwood papers (newsprint),
whenever possible. The trees used are replaced through donations to
the Scoutrees for Canada program. A percentage of all profit is donated
to charitable organizations.

National Library of Canada Cataloguing in Publication Data

Reeves, Nancy Christine, 1952 –
A path through loss

Includes bibliographical references.
ISBN 1-896836-48-8
1. Grief. 2. Spiritual journals – Authorship. I. Title.
BF575.D35R43 2001   152.4   C2001-910829-X

Published by Northstone
an imprint of Wood Lake Books Inc.
Kelowna, British Columbia, Canada
www.joinhands.com

Printing 9 8 7 6 5 4 3 2
Printed in Canada by
Transcontinental Printing

DEDICATION

In gratitude to
my friends
Sophia and Francis
for their wisdom and support

CONTENTS

PART ONE
INTRODUCTION

PART TWO
THE GRIEVING / ADJUSTMENT PROCESS

PART THREE
ISSUES FOR HEALING & GROWTH

PART FOUR
JOURNAL SECTIONS

ACKNOWLEDGMENTS

I am blessed to have a family
who believes in me.
Thank you Tina, Bob, Eric, Pat,
Joan, Rebecca, and Barbara.

Many people gave freely of their
time and energy to read the
manuscript and make helpful suggestions.
Thank you Annette, Jake, Fred,
Luci, Janet, Colin, Linda, Patricia,
Dan, Cele, Garth, and Judi.

And to Mike Schwartzentruber my editor,
and the folks at Northstone,
I greatly appreciate how
you heard and affirmed me
through this joint venture.

PART ONE

INTRODUCTION

Who Am I?

Since 1978, I have, as a clinical psychologist, had the honor of sharing the path through loss with adults and children adjusting to a wide variety of situations. As a psychotherapist and workshop facilitator, I have touched and been touched by thousands of people courageous in their pain.

When I first decided to specialize in the area of trauma, grief, and loss, my colleagues, friends, and family members worried that I would quickly become overwhelmed and burnt out. I felt I was being called to work in this area, yet I respected the concerns of the people who cared about me. So, right from the start, I searched out self-care strategies to keep myself balanced and healthy. Today, I still feel grateful that grieving people include me in their quest for healing and growth.

Why Write Your Grief?

The experience of loss often involves intense emotions, pain, and confusion. Not an easy time to make clear decisions about the most helpful direction for our lives to take. And yet the way we live through loss strongly influences the depth of our healing.

In my clinical practice, I see numerous examples of adults and children who are helped by becoming "informed consumers" of the grieving process. Acquiring information and understanding of themselves and their journey, they experience an empowering which allows them to ride the waves of grief more surely, and to move consciously towards the type of healing or growth that matches their personalities.

Many of these people kept journals prior to encountering their loss. They continue to write afterwards and often read from their journals during our sessions. I have suggested to others that they keep a journal.

Likewise, some people are drawn to courses and workshops when they want to learn more about a topic or be with others who have the same interests or concerns. When these people experience loss, they benefit from grief and loss recovery courses.

Journal writing and attending courses are just two of many aids to help the adjustment process. There is no "correct" strategy, however, so if you feel you would benefit more from just reading this guide, trust yourself. Having said that, if you have never journaled, the following points may encourage you to try.

Benefits of writing

- Writing provides a clear way to see changes, progress, or blocks in your journey.
- Writing is a good way to ensure important insights and decisions are remembered.
- Writing your experiences can allow release of strong emotions.
- Issues often become clearer when written down "in black and white."

Specific benefits of using this book as a journal

- There are many helpful books available that give information about the grieving process. Sometimes my clients tell me that, during journaling, they wonder if a feeling is "normal," or if there is knowledge that would clarify an issue they are exploring. They aren't sure where to find the information they require. I believe that a journal which also provides basic information about the journey through loss provides support on a number of levels.
- I developed some of the models in this guide to respond to client concerns: for example, "How do I know when I'm ready to make a major change after a loss has occurred?" My models have been published in various professional journals, books, and magazines but this is the first time they have been located in one place.
- I frequently hear that it is hard to journal when grieving intensely. One man stated that he wrote "reams and reams of stuff," but later had difficulty finding a particular dream or insight that he wanted to reread. A young woman complained of "writer's block"; filled with emotions,

she couldn't sort out what to write. With sections such as "Blocks" and "Affirmations," this guide provides structure for your writing.

Who Is It For?

This guide is designed for anyone experiencing a loss. It may be used alone or as an adjunct to counseling. You may be grieving one or more of the following.

- Separation or divorce.
- Chronic, life-threatening or terminal illness.
- Unemployment or retirement.
- Loss of culture, relationship, home, etc.
- Loss due to life transitions (such as the "empty nest syndrome," when the kids leave the home).
- Bereavement as a result of the death of a child, before or after birth; of a parent or other family member; a friend, pet, or a public figure for whom you have deep feelings. The death may have been sudden or it may have come after a long process. It may have resulted from accident, illness, suicide, substance overdose, or homicide.

I want to describe a few losses in more detail because the process of grieving them is usually complicated by lowered self-esteem, shame, guilt, a sense of powerlessness, or general ignorance in society.

Traumatic head injury

Many of those I see in psychotherapy have become different people, instantly, through accident or a medical condition such as a stroke. The very tool that would normally help them deal with loss is damaged or gone. This tool consists of the qualities and resources they have developed and learned over the course of their lives.

Every head injury is unique, yet there are many commonalities. Memory problems, slowed thinking, poor concentration, fatigue, inability to handle noise or "busyness," are just a few of the distressing symptoms.

There are also many emotional concerns. As one person said, "My self-esteem went in the trash bin."

An added difficulty is that many people with head injuries do not look damaged. Therefore, others do not offer the support they would for a visible wound, such as a lost limb. People may even judge the injured person, saying, for example, "I also forget at times or feel tired, but I am able to do my job"; they don't realize that these symptoms are vastly more intense and frequent for the person with a head injury.

Survivors of abuse (emotional, physical, sexual, ritual)

This journal may be useful to you, whether you have or have not done a lot of prior exploration of this issue. I have spoken with a number of survivors of abuse who still feel they have unfinished business, even though they have changed many of their attitudes and behaviors and are living in a healthier manner. The unfinished piece for them involves grieving the many losses associated with the abuse: never having a proper childhood or parent, being unable to trust or to enjoy human intimacy, etc.

If you are currently in an abusive relationship, this journal may be a step to finding a way out. No one, no matter how poorly they feel they have acted in the past, deserves to be abused. Abuse diminishes both the abuser and the abused. It is common to feel hopeless and helpless. There is a way out for each person, although it may be extremely difficult, involving other losses. Yet you can't be the growing, nurturing person you were meant to be while being violated and degraded.

After being abused, some people try to change their feelings of powerlessness by becoming abusers themselves. If you have followed this pattern, it can and needs to be stopped. True personal empowerment is found *within*, never by diminishing others. This pattern is hard to break and you need others to help you find life-affirming ways of feeling more potent.

Childhood affected by parental illness or substance abuse

If a parent was or is strongly influenced by past or ongoing physical or mental illness, alcohol or drug abuse, the whole family is in a chronic state of loss and grief. Often, the children take on adult roles to try to keep the family functioning. As adults, we may still feel too responsible for our parents.

Substance abusers

Many people develop a pattern of alcohol or drug (prescribed or recreational) abuse in an attempt to cope with the overwhelming feelings brought on by a loss. Grieving those past losses in a healthier way is an important step to changing the pattern that locks you into substance abuse.

Definitions

Loss

Loss occurs any time you feel diminishment or restriction. At any given point in your personal history, a small or large loss is probably part of the living tapestry of your life. Events we perceive as loss include chronic or life-threatening illness; bereavement; inability to fulfill a dream; separation or divorce; estrangement from a friend, family member, or God; accident; unemployment; and caring for a loved one with special needs.

Grief

Grief involves your total reactions and responses to any loss, not just bereavement. Grieving occurs for some aspects of every major life change. Even extremely positive changes mean some letting go, some goodbyes. By allowing yourself to acknowledge and feel all meanings of a positive change, you can integrate the newness in your life more thoroughly. Part Two, "The Grieving/Adjustment Process" (pp. 23–29), describes grief in more detail.

Healing

Many people carry an unrealistic image of what healing is and how healing happens. As a result, their self-esteem suffers if they are unable to heal in that way.

Healing is not
- Returning totally to a pre-loss status. Even if you had lived the same time period without dealing with a loss, there would have been some changes, positive and negative, in your body, mind, or spirit.
- A guarantee that further loss will not happen to you. Loss is part of the life of the world and humankind.

Healing is
- A shift of energy. The energy that had been used to assist your adjustment to the loss is now freed for your survival and life-enhancement needs.
- Being able to think about the loss without having to "sit" on emotions to keep them from becoming overwhelming.
- Feeling able to live, not just exist.
- A change of focus. The loss leaves the center of your awareness or life. Although at times some aspects of the loss will need time and energy, most of the time it feels integrated in your life.

If you are open to the natural healing that continues both within and beneath the level of awareness and you find ways to enhance and not get in the way of the changes, the result will "fit" you. You may find that healing looks very different from what you had imagined, yet it is just what you needed.

Growth

Growth, as well as healing, is the choice of some. They want to change in some manner, from the way they were prior to the loss. They wish to push past previous limits, enhance personal qualities, learn healthier patterns, or come closer to their image of a "good" human being. Loss shakes up our connections to ourselves and the world, encouraging new ways to see and be.

Is a commitment to growth necessary?

I started my counseling practice with a bias that growth was a necessary adjunct to healing. George changed my beliefs. He was in the final stages of a terminal illness. Most of the people in his life were trying to get him to work through his issues and concerns before he died. I was asked to facilitate this process. As I entered his room, George looked at me, sighed, and said, "I've been this way for 80-odd years. If I were to admit that some of my ways of doing things were wrong, I would feel really bad about my life. I want to just enjoy the rest of my time in peace." We spent our time together talking about helping his family and friends accept this goal. He died shortly after, feeling healed in mind and spirit. We need to respect everyone's right to *choose* healing or growth as a goal.

Strength

I often hear statements such as this: "I wish I could be strong like my friend; she never cries." Strength is not absence of emotion! If you feel something strongly and do not show it, sometimes even to yourself, you are unable to listen to what the feeling is saying about your needs. Unknown needs cannot be met effectively. It is risky to rely on others to meet your needs.

Strength is the ability to acknowledge, clarify, and meet your needs. It is developed by learning to respond both to yourself and to others. The result is "response-able" people. Strength involves flexibility. The rigid tower is smashed to pieces by the hurricane, yet the grasses bend and, although damaged, survive and are renewed.

Some people worry that their emotions "always seem to be getting away" from them. I explore this idea further in Part Two, The Grieving/ Adjustment Process.

How to Use This Guide

This guide is meant to provide a supportive structure as you move through the grieving process. If one of the sections feels restrictive, modify it or scrap it! You may write an essay for each entry or you may find point form useful.

It was not financially feasible to include a large number of blank sheets in each section, nor was it possible to know how big to make each one. One person dreams nightly while another person has one dream a month. So, once some sections are filled, use a blank journal divided into the sections you have found useful. You may want to refer to the information on the adjustment process even after this guide is full, so keep it in the same place as your new journal.

Read the information sections in the guide prior to beginning your writing. Also, each section for writing starts with a few suggestions to help structure your entries.

Goals

Having an idea of your goal on the path through loss will allow you to check your progress more easily. Caring family members, friends, and professional or lay helpers may have goals they want you to accept for yourself. For example, a friend maneuvers you into social situations where you might meet "prospective partners." Or your aunt suggests that you won't be healed until you move, or get a job, or have a child… The list can go on and on.

It is very hard for those who care about you to see you in pain. They have a strong urge to "fix" your problem and are sometimes very forceful in their attempts to have you follow their advice.

What if you follow your friend's goal for you, "just to get her off your back"? If, after some time, you realize that it was a wrong decision for you, resentment will grow. Then you will have a strained relationship and the consequences of an unfortunate decision on top of your other issues.

If the decision turns out to be a beneficial one, an unhelpful belief may be strengthened. It is common during times of loss and stress to think that other people know what's best for you. The belief fosters dependency on others and a lowered self-esteem.

No decision made by a human being is ever 100 percent right or 100 percent wrong. If you are open to learning from your mistakes, you will be able to make decisions without excessive worry about being wrong. I met my husband when I moved to another community to follow the man I thought was the love of my life. That relationship was a disaster. The move was extremely expensive in money, time, and heartache and yet I am so glad I made that decision because, there, I met Bob.

Suggestions for forming a goal for healing or growth

1. **Stay open.** Whatever you decide now, be open to revisions as your needs, desires, or circumstances change. Try not to have a goal that locks you into a narrow lifestyle. Today in your pain, you may say, "My goal is to live a solitary life. I will sell everything and move to a cabin in the woods, never again trusting another to get close to me." As the pain decreases, your feelings may change, but you have taken steps that make a new goal very difficult. Honoring your present feelings and concerns while keeping your options open may result in a short-term goal such as, "I want to simplify my life and have more solitary time. I will rent a cabin for a month to see how that life feels to me."

2. **Take your time.** Stay with a decision long enough to experience where it is leading you. Decision-making consumes time and energy. Changing your mind frequently will confuse and tire you.

3. **Be assertive.** Let others know what your goal is. If they don't agree, thank them for their caring and tell them firmly that you need to follow your own path. Add that you will be open to changing your goal as your situation changes.

4. **Be patient.** Don't expect rapid progress. Remember: grieving takes time and a lot of the healing happens below the level of your awareness.

5. **Trust your process.** It is perfectly natural to have a vague goal at first. If all you can think of is, "I want to feel better," write that down. Over time you will become more specific. "I want to be able to think of Fred without crying," may be your goal after a month. Eventually, you may be able to say, "Because of my loving years with Fred, I know the joy intimate relationships can bring. So I want to enter another loving, intimate relationship when I meet the right person."

6. **Be realistic.** By having a series of short-term goals, you will meet with successes along the path. This can be a lot more encouraging than waiting for a goal that will take years to realize.

7. **Write your goals** in the "New Awareness" section of the journal (p. 109).

PART TWO

THE GRIEVING/ ADJUSTMENT PROCESS

Why Does It Hurt So Much?

Grief hurts. It is a holistic process, involving emotional, physical, spiritual, and mental dimensions. As a result, pain is felt in all these areas. The purpose of the grieving process is to heal, and the pain, strange as it may sound, is helpful to that healing.

A common initial impulse when facing a loss is to ignore it and hope it goes away, or to try to accept it quickly and then attend to something more pleasant. In order to really adjust to a loss, however, it is important to understand not only the fact of the loss, but also the implications and meanings around that fact.

So, for example, if someone receives the diagnosis of a chronic medical condition, at some point they will need to understand and deal with the following implications.

- **Intrapersonal** – What impact does this diagnosis have on their self-esteem and self-image?
- **Interpersonal** – What impact does this diagnosis have on their relationships? Some people become closer; some people end relationships because of illness or other losses. There may be many more people to interact with as medical and other specialists enter the picture.
- **Financial** – How is their financial situation affected? Will changes mean keeping or leaving their home? Will the kids have to forgo important things? Even if the financial situation is improved, there may be problems. Increased money often comes with "strings attached," or other family members may have difficulty with another's increased resources.
- **Roles** – What roles will change or be stopped altogether?
- **Status** – How does being a person with this condition change their position in relation to their family, job, and the wider community? Again, how does this affect their self-image?

- **Physical and psychological status** – We do not come to a grieving situation without a history. There may recently have been a period of stress related to another family member, or work difficulties, or the death of a friend. The impact of these past events will influence resiliency in dealing with the current situation.
- **Time** – Most people say to me, "This loss is bad timing. I wish it weren't happening now!" Of course, a space for loss is never planned. When losses occur, something else has to go or be modified. That "something" may be the purchase of a car or home, a vacation or wedding, adding yet another loss.
- **Type of loss** – Many people believe that this is the most important factor for determining length and depth of grief. Yet this is not borne out by experience. Although losses that seem unnatural, such as the death of a child or a suicide, are often more complex to grieve, it is the *meaning* that the loss holds for a person that will determine the process of adjustment.

Working with implications

By understanding these implications in your life, you can make changes in attitudes and behaviors and adjust to the loss in a way that will allow you to live as fully as possible. This adjustment requires work and many would rather hide in a hole somewhere than put time and energy into grief.

So along come the symptoms that disturb and hurt. They keep you focused on the loss until the work of adjusting is done, just like the physical pain that is present if you gash your arm. This pain is not there to make the experience of the wound even worse; it is a motivator to care for your arm, so that by receiving appropriate medical treatment, the chances of it becoming infected are minimized.

Normal symptoms include but are not limited to:

Emotional
>   sadness
>   anger
>   longing
>   depression
>   anxiety or fear
>   apathy or resignation
>   guilt
>   loneliness

Mental
>   poor concentration
>   poor memory
>   difficulty making decisions

Physical
>   tears
>   sleep disturbance and/or fatigue
>   restlessness
>   weight change
>   diarrhea or constipation
>   cardiovascular disturbance
>   nausea
>   sexual disturbances

Spiritual
>   doubting or examining beliefs
>   sense of distance from God
>   difficulty praying or meditating

These symptoms tend to be more frequent and intense during the first few months of the grieving process. Later, that they may again become stronger as a new implication is worked through.

If the grieving process is allowed, it comes and goes in waves. We move in and out of various implications and symptoms as they become relevant. Each member of a family will have different grief experiences. One person feels anger when the company lays him off while another feels anxious about the family's financial situation.

By riding the waves, we do not stay long in very intense grief. Some people have a problem feeling deeply and try to keep busy or to otherwise divert themselves. Others feel guilty when they have the normal "respite" periods where they feel little grief, and so they think or feel themselves back to a deep level. Interfering with the natural process by trying to control the depth of grief is exhausting and slows the process.

When our grief is particularly intense, we may feel like a rudderless ship. We have no direction and no interest in finding one. Although this feeling is very normal and will pass, it helps to have some kind of structure during this time. Routine can feel comforting, or at least ensure that we eat and rest. Even if we can't sleep, lying in bed allows the body time to rest and replenish resources, and gives the mind and emotions much-needed quiet space.

Children, especially, need routine during the grieving process. School, sleepovers with friends, sports, and other activities can feel like emotional anchors in the chaos of grief. Don't force routine on yourself or others, however. A great deal of energy is going into the healing process so it is impossible to keep the same pre-loss routine.

Early on, and then periodically throughout the grieving process, you may find yourself numb or not taking in the reality of the loss or an implication of it. It is as if you are emotionally anesthetized. This experience is protective, for if the full impact of the loss or impending loss hit all at once, it would be emotional and physical overload. So your system holds your grief, letting it out at an intensity you can handle.

How Long Does It Last?

"All right, so grieving is normal. I'll take a week off and deal with all the implications and then I'll be healed." Unfortunately, no process works like that. Otherwise you could eat all the food you need for a week at one meal.

The grieving process is like a spider web. Every strand is connected, yet we can't tell beforehand which strand will be more appropriate to travel on. One implication may not be grieved for years. For example, telling a young widow to grieve the fact that her husband will not be present to give his daughter away in marriage makes no sense. Fifteen years later, as she prepares for the wedding, the mom may grieve. If she knows this is normal, the grief can actually feel like a meaningful connection with her child's natural father.

Significant dates or situations often result in an upsurge of grieving symptoms. The term for this is "anniversary reaction." The symptoms usually move off quite quickly if they are allowed expression. Anniversary reactions are often expected at times such as birthdays or the date the loss occurred.

Some, however, catch us off guard. Personally meaningful times, such as the first snowfall or reaching the same age that our father was when he died, may bring on strong surges of grief. If you experience an unexpected intense emotion, ask yourself what is currently happening in your life that could be connected to the loss.

No one can tell how long your grieving process will last since they don't know how many implications need to be grieved. Other than the beginning of grief when you are "eating, breathing, and sleeping" your loss, the waves of the grieving process do allow periods when the loss sits lighter. You may even feel happy at times.

PART THREE

ISSUES FOR
HEALING
& GROWTH

Energy Management

Many grieving people say to me, "Why have I had such little energy since I started dealing with this loss? I need my energy now more than ever!" I developed the Energy Management Model in the early 1980s to answer this question. Many grieving people have the same amount of energy they have always had: it is just being used differently. Other people, because of energy-sapping chronic illness or traumatic head injury, have less energy. Using your energy efficiently and effectively will help the healing process.

I define "energy" as the force that allows us to be and think and do. Energy can be viewed as a circle. Some have bigger circles than others, but for everyone energy is finite. Going past energy limits means needing more rest later.

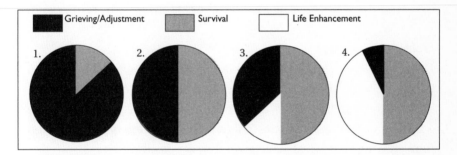

Circle 1: When a loss is first felt, most of our energy is used for grieving/readjustment. We eat, breathe, and sleep our loss. A much smaller slice is used for survival activities. We need help to survive, however. If food is put in front of us, we eat, but have no energy or interest in preparing a meal.

Circle 2: As time passes and we work through our grief, we reach a point where all energy needed for survival is available. We still use a lot of energy for grieving. People often feel discouraged at this time because they think they are regressing: "I feel worse now than I did a few weeks (or months) ago." They are actually progressing, but with the emotional anesthetic wearing off, they feel the loss more intensely.

Circle 3: When a little life enhancement begins to emerge, many people experience it coming almost overnight. They wake up feeling lighter in spirit. Instead of visiting a friend only to receive support, they are interested in their friend's life. The loss does not color their whole world anymore. There is energy for play.

Circle 4: This process continues until there is only a small slice of energy being used for grieving. This slice never leaves, yet it is not restrictive. In fact, tapping into it can produce warm memories and feelings of connection.

People do not move through this model in a sequential manner. As new implications or intense emotions are experienced, we will move back and forth through the circles. Couples, families, and communities who are grieving together will find members in differing places in their use of energy. Remember: we all have unique responses to the same event.

Using the model

Deciding when to make a major move after a loss can be difficult. Becoming pregnant again, leaving the family home, changing jobs, or entering a new relationship, all take tremendous energy. Where do we get this energy? If we are in the first two circles, the energy will be taken from grieving or survival, which will slow our healing.

In some cases this is acceptable to us. Sue, who's in her mid-40s, told me, "I know it's very soon after my baby's death to get pregnant again, but that biological time clock is ticking and there will be more problems if I wait." Even trying to become pregnant takes physical, mental, emotional, and spiritual energy. Taking from our grieving energy can make for trouble later. Grief will begin again, intensely, at inappropriate times such as at the birth of the new child. Instead, it is better to find energy for the new undertaking from survival and see if there are any aspects of survival that can be dropped, for example, working part time and delegating other needs to family and friends.

Many people feel the first freedom of life enhancement and get busy with some major change. Unfortunately, they quickly use up this energy, feel trapped, and resent the new activity. We can see this in the rebound effect after a relationship breaks up.

Joe tells me for months, "I will never, ever get into another relationship." Then, one morning, he awakens feeling like a load has been lifted off his shoulders. He enjoys his breakfast and the crisp feel and smell of the winter air. He whistles on the way to work. Later, Joe sees a woman in a store who smiles at him. He smiles back and thinks, "I actually feel something for this person. It must be love." Basing a new relationship on the initial feelings of life enhancement is not a good move. Joe is likely headed for another fall.

Waiting for some time between the third and fourth circle will allow energy for the major change to be taken from life enhancement, with some left for play. A number of people have used the circles to monitor their energy usage and to decide when they are ready for the change.

People with chronic illness or traumatic head injury tend to have smaller energy circles. Those who care daily for a family member with special needs may find that their survival needs are so great they never have much life enhancement energy. These situations call for creativity.

Rachel, who spent much of her days taking her son with special needs to medical and rehabilitation appointments, became angry with me in the parent group I was facilitating: "There is no way I can find any time for life enhancement!" I replied that I trusted her determination and creativity, which was present when she met an obstacle to do with her beloved child. I asked her to use those qualities to care for herself and suggested a number of questions that would help her clarify what life-enhancing activity would be meaningful and do-able.

1. What qualities/gifts are within me that are not being used enough or at all?

2. What personal dreams (realistic or unrealistic, from childhood and adulthood) have not come to fruition?
3. What expensive emotions are weighing me down? (These are described in the section on "Complicated Grief," p. 71.)
4. What attracts or interests me?

The next steps, I suggested, were to look at her answers and pull out a theme, such as "creativity" or "learning"; choose an activity that will meet some aspect of this theme; allow herself to be flexible so that the activity is "do-able"; and act on this as soon as possible.

After hearing all this, Rachel said that it wasn't possible and stomped out of the group.

Two weeks later she was back and asked to speak first. After letting go of her anger, Rachel had pondered the questions. Her answers indicated a need to do something to manifest her creativity. So Rachel went to a craft store and asked for a project that would fit in her purse, be unbreakable, and be easy for someone who had never done a craft. The owner sold her a simple cross-stitch design for a cushion. Rachel did her cross-stitch while she waited for appointments and was able to do a significant amount in two weeks.

Rachel proudly showed us her work and said, "I have never thought of myself as creating beautiful things. Now, instead of complaining with the other parents about how long the waiting is, we talk about my craft. I even had one pediatrician admire my cushion and ask how I ever found the time to do it. I told him, 'Waiting for you, Doctor'. He was actually embarrassed and we got in quicker next time."

It is not always possible to tell whether an activity is survival or life enhancement without asking about the need it is meeting. For example, early in my grief, I would probably ignore my physical appearance for a few days. My 16-year-old daughter would head right for the bathroom to put on makeup. For me, grooming is life enhancement; for a teenager, it is survival.

The journal section "Energy Movement" includes a number of blank circles to help you monitor your status.

Children's Experience with Loss

It is not possible to move through life without encountering loss. Some of us go through long stretches where life seems to consist of one loss after another. It can be useful to understand how our past has affected us, because grieving styles are learned and can be changed. We will explore how to change these patterns later in this book.

I often begin workshops on children and grief by talking about my daughter Tina's favorite bedtime story when she was three. You know, the story that your child requests night after night. The one they have memorized, so that even though they can't read yet, they know if you leave out one word.

Tina's story involved a little fellow who was nearly murdered by the person who had killed his father. After a number of hair-raising escapes, our hero got safely home. I ask the group if they read stories like this to their preschoolers. At this point many members of the audience shake their heads "no," look concerned, and glance towards the door. When I tell them the name of this "horrific" book, *The Tale of Peter Rabbit* by Beatrix Potter, the response is quick: "My child loves that book. It's about cute little rabbits, not death!"

Yet if you ask any preschooler, "What happened to Peter's daddy?" the response is, "Mr. McGregor killed him and baked him in a pie. He'd kill Peter if he could catch him." Children do not love this story for the violence. They love it because it makes them feel secure to know that even though Peter was disobedient and went where he was told not to go, he was still loved and comforted by his mom when he returned. Peter had to pay the consequence for his actions: being put to bed and taking chamomile tea because he caught a cold hiding in a watering can half full of water. Yet the love was not taken away.

Children are often much more realistic about loss than adults are. And they watch us to see how to heal. Is showing and sharing feelings and concerns acceptable? Why is there loss and grief? Although implications and intensity will vary from loss to loss, each of us tends to follow the style of grieving we learned as we were growing up.

Children's understanding of the world changes as they grow through developmental stages. So does their understanding of loss. If children experience losses without receiving support, they may become "stuck" at the stage where the loss occurred and grieve any future loss in that way.

For example, a young child naturally has concerns about being abandoned, that significant adults will emotionally or physically withdraw. Sometimes adults feel they are protecting children by not telling them about a loss. Children, being very sensitive to the "vibes" in a home, realize something is wrong and become worried without receiving support for their distress. The child who associates loss with abandonment will tend to view loss in future life as "being left alone."

Two normal aspects of childhood play a large part in how a child views loss. The first is "egocentrism" – the child believes they are the center of the universe and views any situation from an intensely personal viewpoint. "Gramma died because I didn't send a thank-you letter for the gift she gave me." Egocentrism is very strong in early childhood, then diminishes, only to increase again in adolescence. It is more visible during times in a child's growth where many changes are occurring in body and mind. By focusing so intently on self, the child is able to more easily monitor and integrate this newness. It is very common for four- and 14-year-olds to respond similarly to news of a loss. "How does this affect *me?*" If adults know this is normal, they will help the child feel secure by meeting their need for security. Then other implications of the loss will be able to be grieved.

The second common developmental principle is the need to create order out of disorder in our world. Children are not content with being told, "Wait, you'll understand when you're older." When something concerns them, they will search out knowledge. If the adults won't talk about it, the nine-year-old neighbor will. Unfortunately, children don't have the life experience and mental maturity to piece bits of information together correctly. Watch two-year-olds playing with a jigsaw puzzle. If a piece does not fit, they may "solve" the problem by biting some of it off to make it smaller. Young children may use the same strategy with situations, such as loss, that are unfamiliar. The resulting misinformation may frighten and con-fuse more than the reality. When adults are willing to talk openly about loss in front of their children, the young ones can revise this misinformation.

A young child's world is very concrete: "Love is getting a hug." It is only in adolescence that our brains can handle abstract concepts: "Love is the mystical bond between two souls!" (Something I expe-rience but my parents never did.) Concrete-thinking children often worry that we continue to function biologically after death: "It's pretty cold outside and my dog is buried without a blanket," or "Won't crema-tion hurt her?"

I calm the child's fears in the following way. Holding a piece of their hair, I gently tug it and ask, "Can you feel that?"

"Yes."

"That's because your hair is attached to the part of you that feels."

Then, with the child's permission, I gently pull out or cut off a strand of their hair. Holding each end, I pull. "Does that hurt?"

Preschoolers may take some seconds to think. "Nope, it doesn't."

As I burn an end, "Does that hurt?"

"No."

I bury the strand in the ground and invite the child to jump on the "grave." "Does that hurt?"

"Nope."

"It is still your hair, although it isn't attached to the part of you that feels anymore, so it doesn't have life in it. When someone dies, the part that feels goes out of the body and what's left is just like that strand of hair. It doesn't feel or grow. Without life, it may start to change, to come apart, like that old apple core we found under your bed.

"There are many ways to remember someone who has died. We can look at photographs, go to places they liked, think or talk about them and do something with their body that will help our memories. Some people want their bodies buried in a place where people can come to think about them. Others want to be cremated and have their ashes scattered to provide nutrients for nature to use. We know now that it doesn't hurt the body."

Other issues to keep in mind when helping children

- Their sense of time. Adults struggle with the concept of eternity. A child who knows three "sleeps" may wait a week, "an eternity," before asking if it's time to move back to their former home.
- Older children (ages five to nine) go through a stage of "magical thinking." They believe that their thoughts are so powerful, they can make their wishes come true. They may feel responsible for parents' separation: "I wished they would stop fighting and then Daddy moved out." The child may be ashamed to tell us about their guilt. If a child suddenly changes behavior after a loss, either becoming very clinging or withdrawn, they may be feeling guilt.

  Magical thinking is normal and you can't talk a child "out of it." You can, however, provide information. "Thoughts are very powerful, yet we need thoughts *and* actions to make something happen. If I sit on a swing and wish it to move, nothing happens. If I ask someone for a push or use my own body, I will get my ride." Children need to know that we do not hold them responsible for a loss.

  Sometimes children ask about prayer as "evidence" that thoughts make things happen. It is not our own mind that answers prayer. Prayer is a dialogue, not a monologue.
- It is normal that as older children and adolescents form deeper connections with their peers, they may go to them for support more often than to their parents.
- Teenagers have a "personal fable" that encourages them to feel invulnerable: "I knew someone else would crash the car at that speed, but I really knew my car and didn't think I'd lose control." Personal loss may come as a shock and be viewed as unnatural. Adolescents also experience the "imaginary audience," the belief that others are watching them, either with approval or judgment. There is a great need to fit into the peer group and grieving may be seen as making them appear different. With information about the grieving process, teens can encourage their friends to share their pain and be more willing to allow their own grief.

- Children's understanding of loss and grief is also shaped by television, books, other adults and peers, faith, and school. By inviting children to share their questions and concerns with us, we can understand how these factors are influencing them.

Clarify your own grief history. You may find it useful to list the losses you have experienced in your lifetime in the "New Awareness" section. Ordering your losses by the age you were when they occurred and noting their impact on you gives a picture of your grief history. Ask yourself the following questions: What message did the significant adults in my life give me about grief and loss? How did the significant adults in my life grieve? Whose style of grief did I take on? How does my style help and hinder my adjustment process?

Even losses that you were too young to remember will have affected your feelings, attitudes, and behaviors. As you think about each loss, see if you can identify how it is carried into your present. We often give ourselves messages at the time of a loss that we continue to accept without examination for the rest of our lives. Sometimes these messages give us hope and trust in our ability to deal well with future losses, and sometimes they restrict our lives and make us anxious.

An example of the first message, after the death of a friend, could be, "Our relationship was precious to me and it is worth the pain I feel now to have had such a friend." A restrictive message would be something like, "It hurts so much because I loved so much. So I'm never going to love anyone as deeply again. Then I'll never be hurt." This message encourages shallow, unsatisfying relationships throughout life.

Tips for helping children

- Basic helping strategies are the same for adults and children and are described in the section "Helping Others" (p. 73).
- Letting children see our grief teaches them that strong emotions are normal and that sharing concerns with others feels supportive and allows needs to be met. Children know all about strong emotions –

watch any two-year-old having a tantrum – and they look to us to learn how to express them in acceptable ways.

- Children's beliefs and values are shaped by the way their family adjusts to loss. Look at the verbal and non-verbal messages you give the children in your life. You may be familiar with the large bronze sculptures of artist Henry Moore. Many pieces are abstract human figures done in a very simplified style. When Henry was a child, his mother, who had chronic back pain, was often bedridden. Henry used to massage cream over the curves of her sore back. Instead of restricting him, the experience of caring for his mother was translated, years later, into his rounded sculptures that invite our touch.

- Watch the words you use with children. Young ones take our words literally. It is no wonder that after hearing that Grandma is now "at rest," a young child becomes anxious when told it is his or her naptime. Explaining how a word can have different meanings, and asking a child what a word she uses means to her, can help us see if a term is being misconstrued. Using euphemisms, such as "passed away" and "lost my job" will confuse rather than soften the loss for children, unless we explain the meaning of these phrases.

- After experiencing a loss, children and adults will often regress to a time they felt the world was safe and good. Baby talk, using a bottle again, or the need for more physical reassurance, is normal. Children will feel more secure if you allow them these comforts. The urge for growth is strong and soon they will again be acting their chronological age.

Spirituality

Increasing numbers of people are looking for a direction in life that includes deep, responsive relationships with others, with the earth and its creatures, and with the divine. During times of loss, the need for direction can become desperately important, as an attempt to make sense of pain and suffering.

Spirituality is our personal response to life's mysteries and questions. It is how we open to and engage with the spirit of the divine.

Religion provides a structure for spirituality. It consists of clarified beliefs and laws. Various groups or denominations within a religion may interpret some of these beliefs and laws differently, but the core beliefs are the same. Those who identify with a particular religion need spirituality to make their beliefs live.

During grief, we question the four "core" or ultimate concerns described by philosophers as:

- **Mortality** – the inescapable fact that we and those we love, will die.
- **Isolation** – Existential isolation is the realization that no other person or creature can ever bridge the gap and unite with us in our feelings, thoughts, and actions. They can come close, but when we experience existential isolation "a miss is as good as a mile."
- **Freedom** – Existential freedom can be exhilarating and terrifying. It is the concept that we have the free will to *be* and act in positive or negative ways. There is no ultimate structure that controls us. This responsibility for ourselves means we are constantly choosing between options.

  Even refusing to choose is a choice! I am told often by grieving people, "There was no choice; it was the only thing to be done." There are always choices, yet we often ignore or are blind to them. The other options may be so life destroying, so far from our beliefs and values that we don't even look at them. By realizing we always have choices, we can be more receptive to seeing other, positive options that might be unfamiliar.

- **Meaninglessness** – What is the meaning of life? With the freedom to choose, each of us needs to find and live the meaning that is a match for us. Parents consciously or unconsciously teach their children the meaning they live. Religions teach the meaning they believe the divine wants us to follow. Advertising agencies make millions by linking products to positive meanings. We can exist but cannot *live* without meaning.

At this point, I want to clarify my own beliefs. I am in awe of the diversity in this world. A few different kinds of birds would have been sufficient, yet we are surrounded by an incredible richness of sizes, shapes, and colors. This lavishness of creation extends to human beings.

I believe that the paths to the Intelligence who created this diversity are also many and varied. As creatures of structure, we try to name this Source of our being. YHWH, the Goddess, God, Allah, Life, the Divine, are only a few. Naming implies that our stance towards this Being is one of relationship. When we can honor and celebrate the words and paths others use, I believe it sets our image of the divine free of the rigid containers that names can be.

Some of us find that traditional paths, with their well-defined years of tradition, provide us the most support and direction. Some of us feel a deeper connection with the divine on "new age" paths. Our way may be solitary or within a large faith community. My own path is a Christian one.

Repeatedly, the texts of many faith traditions speak of the divine loving and wanting a deep relationship with us. When we encounter pain and loss, it is natural to wonder about its presence in our lives and how a connection to our Source could help us. The following questions and concerns are ones I hear often.

What if I have no beliefs?

Everyone has beliefs, although they may be unexamined. When I ask grievers, "What are the qualities that make a 'good' person?" they always have an answer. Clarifying your ideas and feelings about this question, and others, can make your beliefs more conscious. "What meaning have I given to my life and do I want to keep that meaning?" "How would I describe the divine?" The benefit of conscious beliefs is an increase in self-esteem and a feeling of becoming part of the divine plan as you perceive it.

I long for something but have been hurt by religion

Many injustices have been committed in the name of religion. You may have been abused or restricted by a person or faith community who justified their actions by quoting religious texts. It is so easy to twist or misinterpret words. All religions face the challenge of being true to their origins while responding to a changing culture and understanding of human psychology and needs. If you have left the religion you grew up with, due to bad experiences, and yet desire a faith structure, there are a number of directions you can take.

First, clarify your beliefs. It may be easier if someone assists you. Read "Self-Care" (p. 61). Next, examine the religion that has been hurtful to you. Separating the beliefs from the people who harmed you can be freeing. You may find you still "fit" this tradition. Because I have contact with people in various faiths, I sometimes arrange meetings so that a client can vent anger and hurt and ask questions about how the religion has changed over the years.

In exploring the beliefs of your former religion, you may find you are on a different track and need to look elsewhere for a "fit." Attending services, talking to members of different faiths, reading sacred texts, helps you find the one that is a good match.

Why does God allow pain and suffering?

Joyce Rupp, in her excellent book *Praying Our Goodbyes*, lists four common incorrect beliefs about pain and suffering.

1. God sends these experiences out of love for us.
2. God is punishing us for some sin by sending us suffering.
3. God is testing our faith through pain.

4. Pain is God's will, which is beyond our understanding.

These beliefs have added much misery to our grief, because, we reason, if God wants us to have this pain, then what right have we to stop it?

All faith traditions that speak of a Creator, describe that Being as loving and compassionate. The divine does not want us to suffer, yet the only way God can prevent suffering is to intervene directly. This would destroy our free will and make us little more than puppets. Although it would feel wonderful to have God intervene in the bad times, we would always question how much our lives were being controlled.

Birth and death, growth and decay, loss and gain, health and illness are all aspects of the life cycle. Hurricanes and droughts are consequences of natural forces, although with our human history of plundering the earth, we contribute to a number of "natural disasters." The archaic, misguided belief that they are "acts of God" survives primarily in the language of insurance policies.

My friend cannot take away my pain, but knowing she is willing to stand beside me in love and acceptance makes it easier for me to bear my burden. If we change our notion of a punitive, judging God to an image of a Friend who suffers with us and who wants us to live happy, fulfilled lives, we can feel comfort and gain courage to meet life's losses.

Is God only found in church?

Remember the most awesome experiences of your life, when you felt intense love, connectedness, joy, or gratitude. Examples could be holding your newborn child or grandchild, gazing into your friend's eyes and knowing you are loved unconditionally, a sunset that caused your soul to sing, or feeling communion with others as you filled sandbags to keep the rising river from destroying your homes. At these times you had experience of the divine.

Many people, who are intentionally on a spiritual path, search for ways to have these awe-inspiring experiences more often. Although

ISSUES FOR HEALING AND GROWTH ~ 47

God is not just present in church, some seekers find that worshipping together builds an intensity of feeling and gives a sense of supportive community.

How does grief affect beliefs?

It is extremely common and natural to doubt our beliefs for some time during grief. Even knowing that the divine did not cause our loss, we can feel angry and abandoned. If we allow ourselves our feelings, most of us will move slowly to an even clearer set of beliefs, and live them more richly. Many then say, "Now I know loss can happen at any time, so I want to live as fully as possible."

They tell me to "give it to God"

A time comes when anger, pain, or bitterness restricts us and needs to be released. A common suggestion is to "Give it to God." Many people find that when they attempt to do this, they feel freer for a while. Then the feeling or concern returns. This is due to our patterns of attitudes and behaviors that magnify, resonate with, or attract these feelings and concerns. True freedom comes when we give the feeling or concern and ourselves to the divine and work in partnership to transform these patterns.

What about evil?

Few people want to think or speak about the subject of evil. Yet grieving people are sometimes very vulnerable to harm from evil. Death, pain, and loss are normal, natural parts of the cycle of life. Yet most of us have had at least one experience in our lives of encountering a person or a place that created a hopeless, sick feeling. Or we have read or heard of torture or other suffering inflicted with a sense of enjoyment. William Bloom, in his book *Psychic Protection*, defines evil acts as "destruction with no creative purpose."

There are many views about the source of evil: some people see it as coming from a supernatural being; other people think of it as an energy field created by centuries of cruelty. Regardless of our religious or spiritual beliefs about the source of evil, if we feel its presence we need to learn how to deal with it. There are many practical techniques for balancing, grounding and protecting yourself when faced with the normal "bad vibes" of living, such as an argument with your boss, as well as with abnormal experiences of evil.

Representatives of various faiths stress the following:

- Some people in their "woundedness" act in harmful ways. This doesn't make them evil. They can, with help, change their attitudes and behaviors and live in healthy, growing ways.
- If you encounter what you believe to be evil, do not try to deal with it alone. Don't try to "fix" evil. It is too old and too big. Tap into your beliefs for the strongest supernatural force for good you know and ask for help and protection.
- There are people in every faith who have training and experience in this area who are available for consultation.

Spiritual tools

There are a great variety of spiritual tools we can use to help us interact with the divine. It is possible to discover techniques done alone or with others, in stillness or with movement, in silence or with much loudness, with simplicity or with splendiferous pomp. Even when selecting one tool such as prayer, we find a large number of types. Explore and experiment until you find a few that work for you. Spiritual tools usually become more effective with use; changing them constantly can limit their effectiveness.

The journal section "Spiritual Issues" gives you space to examine your beliefs. The following two issues, "Forgiveness" and "Guilt," are related to our beliefs and arise for many people during the grieving process.

Forgiveness

Forgiveness is a thorny, complicated issue. We forgive when we cease to resent. We may still feel angry or sad that the experience occurred and acknowledge that the other person did something that caused us injury. If we believe that the other may act the same way in the future, we find ways to protect ourselves and may also encourage the other to change. Forgiving does not mean staying in an abusive situation.

The way of forgiveness leads to release of the feelings of bitterness, hate, or vengeance that keep us from healing. Refusing to forgive keeps those anxiety producing feelings very much in our awareness. You may know people whose lives revolve around their hate or need for vengeance.

I believe vengeance is the most seductive drug we have, because it gives the illusion of power and strength. It is so stimulating that it takes a lot of our energy. Vengeance pushes for action and that action is always towards violence. Violence just begets more violence in ourselves and others.

Expecting that another will continue to act in wrong ways often contributes to that happening. I remember an incident years ago when I worked as a day-care supervisor. On John's first day, his mom told me in his hearing that he did not get on well with others. Later that day, three-year-old John hit another child. I told him that hurting other people is not acceptable and he stated in his mom's voice, "I don't get along with other kids." John did, in fact, have a problem with anger. But labeling him as an aggressive child gave an identity that not only permitted violent behavior, but made it an expectation.

Being peaceable, on the other hand, is not being apathetic, resigning, or giving in to oppression or violence. It also pushes for action. Working for peace means forgiving and healing the wounded parts of ourselves, others, and our world, so that wrongdoing is less likely.

If you feel you have never committed an intentional or unintentional wrong against another person, this section may be irrelevant to you. I, however, and I imagine most of us, feel remorse for speaking or refusing to speak, acting or refusing to act in a way that restricted or violated another.

To forgive you need to do the following.

- Forgive yourself. The next section on guilt describes a process for doing this. If we continue to blame ourselves for past wrongs, we squander energy that could be used for living in nurturing, responsive ways. We diminish ourselves and this impacts negatively on those around us. If we can't forgive ourselves, we will not be able to forgive others.

- Clarify the "feeling" of forgiveness. The following exercise may help. Think back to a time when you were forgiven, and a time when you forgave another. It doesn't matter if the wrongdoing was tiny or life changing. Remember it in detail – how you felt, what you thought, what you and the other did.

  See if you can identify the internal process you went through that allowed you to forgive. Similarly, see if you can identify the process that allowed you to accept forgiveness. You may find it useful to remember these incidents as you encounter a new situation where forgiveness is called for. Write your insights in "New Awareness."

- Clarify your beliefs about justice. We may think that we don't often encounter justice issues in our lives. In reality, we deal with them on a daily basis. Mediating a disagreement between our children, signing a petition, deciding whether to grab the parking spot someone else has been waiting for – all these situations call for us to think in justice terms.

  Examine your reaction when someone does wrong to you. If you blame automatically and wish to punish the other, you hold a punitive justice orientation. A transformative or restorative justice stance wants the wrongdoing to be resolved in a way that brings healing and reparation for you, and a change in attitudes and behaviors towards remorse and rehabilitation for the offender. When you think of your goal for the wrongdoing, it may help to ask yourself, "What do I want resolution to look like: now? next week? next year? etc." A punitive approach usually is a "quick fix" for immediate feelings and concerns, without providing increased chances for long-term safety.

- Look to see who else you are blaming. We often hold others partially responsible for not preventing the wrongdoing or for not dealing with it effectively or efficiently. Commonly we blame a family member, the divine, society, the justice system, or a friend. If we forgive the offender but not these others, we still hold restricting resentment.

- Making a statement of forgiveness can be a powerful part of your resolution. Activities such as meeting with the offender in a healing circle, or writing a letter, gives you the opportunity to express your pain, make suggestions for reparation, and show that you forgive.

Guilt

A large percentage of people feel guilt, at times, in their grieving process. Intensity can range from mild regret to paralyzing guilt, where we feel we will never be able to live with our actions or lack of actions that contributed to the loss.

Actually, I see guilt as a positive and useful emotion that is not used correctly. Guilt is a motivator; it asks us to look at an unwanted situation and decide what changes we need to make in our attitudes and/or behaviors in order to live safer and healthier, now and in the future.

Unfortunately, those who are guilt-ridden tend to accept total responsibility for the past and punish themselves unendingly. Self-punishment contributes to a diminishing of self, so the person has few resources to give to others and the world. So punishment, instead of setting things right, adds more loss and pain to the griever and to friends and family who become increasingly worried.

A three-step process

I help people work through their guilt in three steps. Many find their guilt leaves after the first step and there is no need to continue. Others need to complete all three steps. Whether the guilt is rational or irrational has little to do with its strength or how easily we work through it. I frequently hear, "I know this guilt is not rational, but I can't seem to let it go." If talking yourself out of the guilt is going to work, as it has for a number of people, it will happen quite quickly. These three steps are for those people for whom guilt hangs on.

For these steps to be effective, it is important to put time and energy into them. When someone says to me, "I feel guilty," I usually respond with, "Good, I like working with people who have a conscience."

Remember:

- It is what you do with it, not the guilt itself that is the problem.
- It is not possible to return to the past and prevent a wrong from occurring. It is possible to change ourselves so that we are more potent forces for good in the world. A guilt-ridden person spreads little light.

Step One: Hear what the guilt is saying to you and bring it out in the open

Take time to explore all the aspects of the loss you feel guilty about. Write them down. Some people find it useful to rate their intensity on a five- or ten-point scale. Talk to at least one other person about your guilt. Ask them to listen without trying to talk you out of it. Their listening will break the circle of shame-filled secrecy that locks us into our guilt. You may also find some aspects coming clearer as you tell someone else. Their questions may open up an area of which you were unaware. Also tell them that you are making a commitment to resolve your guilt.

If you believe you have wronged another person, this is the time to tell them you feel remorse for your part in their pain. Many cultures and religions have developed rituals, such as the First Nations healing circle or the Roman Catholic confession, to structure the process for letting go of guilt.

For many people, acknowledging and clarifying their feelings of guilt allows the guilt to leave. You are honoring your feeling of connection to the loss without needing to accept full inappropriate responsibility. You become aware of what changes in attitudes and behaviors you need to commit to.

Jesse's story: Jesse, a man in his late 60s, realized he felt guilt about the amount of time his adult children gave to him after the death of his wife. In exploring his guilt, he had two insights. First, he needed to modify his independent attitude a little to allow himself to gracefully accept their gift of attention. By grudgingly taking the help, he had been belittling their love.

Second, he realized he needed to pay more attention to his friendships. A close, mutual support system of peers would meet his needs in a way that was more acceptable to him.

Step Two: Education or re-education

Read and add to your entry on guilt until you find it diminishing, or you realize more is needed. Sometimes step one brings to light a weak area in our ways of responding to life. The guilt will remain until this has been rectified.

Mari's story: Mari's young son died in the backyard after being stung by a bee, as she was at the front trying to close the door on a salesperson. Even if she had been present, she may not have been able to save her child, as no one knew of his extreme allergy. Yet Mari knew that her nonassertiveness had kept her from returning to him more quickly. After clarifying all her guilt, she decided to take an assertiveness training course and a first-aid course.

Other examples of education and re-education include entering a process of psychological or spiritual counseling, and taking appropriate courses such as anger management, parenting, financial management, life skills, or defensive driving.

Step Three: Reconciliation

Once the learning that we committed to as a way to be more responsive and responsible in the world is complete, the guilt may move off. It often disappears over time as the changes brought by the learning sink in, so it is useful to wait for some weeks or months before starting on step three.

The step of reconciliation is a voluntary giving of ourselves, demonstrating the depth of our remorse. Punishment diminishes the person who feels guilt as well as those connected with him or her. Reconciliation is different; for it to be successful, everyone involved needs to have the opportunity to heal and grow.

Read the next section on ritual before deciding on the most appropriate activity. If another was involved in the loss, ask them for ideas. If this is not possible, talk to someone who knew them.

Richard's story: Richard thought he could drive safely while drunk. He struck and severely injured ten-year-old Amy. Richard wanted to do self-directed reconciliation on top of that prescribed by the courts. His reconciliation involved writing a letter to Amy and her parents and then meeting with them and their pastor.

He told them of the commitment he had made through AA to stop drinking and he asked what else he could do. Amy's mom told him that their small hospital had to import blood for her daughter, so Richard decided to become a blood donor. He would donate ten times to match Amy's ten years.

An "end of sentence"

It is important when choosing an activity for reconciliation to have "an end of sentence." If you feel locked into an activity, it will become "duty" and those you are helping will sense that your heart is no longer in it. Choosing a symbolic time as Richard did can make the activity more potent. Richard decided to continue to give blood after the ten times, because it had been so satisfying. He sent a card to Amy, telling her he had kept his commitments and then continued the activity for himself.

Some people find that a ceremony to mark the end of a reconciling activity useful. Examples of reconciling activities include entering a program to help you stop smoking, volunteer work associated with the loss, raising money for charity.

Note: The other person may choose not to accept your apology or invitation to reconcile. This is their right and you are not responsible for their choice. If they choose to remain angry or judgmental, it is still important to go through the process of reconciling with yourself and then let your guilt go.

Ritual

Stories of our journey through loss often include rituals, ceremonies that attempt to ease the pain. I discovered very early in my work that people are rarely neutral about rituals. They either told me how very helpful the ceremony was, "The concentrated love and caring at the funeral were so intense, I was carried by the memory over the next few grief-filled weeks," or the experience hindered the adjustment process: "What a stupid, hypocritical service! Hard chairs, uncomfortable clothes, the pastor calling him Frederick. It was all the exact opposite of who Freddy was!"

I became interested in the elements that contribute to a ritual being helpful or harmful. For the major research paper in my doctoral program, I intensively studied five people who had felt "stuck" in their grief and used some type of ritual to help them move towards healing and growth.

What is a ritual?

All cultures throughout history have developed rituals to mark important events and to help people through transitions. The anthropologist van Gennep talks about three types of rituals for times of transition. Each type of ritual helps us cross a threshold. He views these times as crossing a threshold. The Latin word for threshold is *limen*.

Taking a family member's death as the transition, the three types of rituals could be as follows.

- **Preliminal** – preparing for the death – writing a will, gathering family and friends at the bedside.
- **Liminal** – the actual transition – cleaning the body; holding a wake, funeral, or service.
- **Postliminal** – letting go of the status of "griever" or moving past the phase of intense grief – no longer wearing mourning clothes, scattering the ashes after some months, conducting a potlatch.

A ritual is a ceremony that marks a significant experience. It is seen as out-of-the-ordinary and contains deep, often sacred meaning and emotion. It is not ritualized behavior, those habits we develop, such as the first cup of coffee watching the sunrise, or the after-dinner stroll. These ritualized behaviors can be very comforting for us and without them it may be harder to heal.

Rituals, though, take us out of our normal lives, inviting us to a closer, purer connection with ourselves, our world, and that source of all that is, which some call God, Life, the Divine, Allah, Mother. This process encourages us to stretch our limits and to change unhelpful attitudes, beliefs, and behaviors.

Benefits of ritual

If ritual is done well, it can help us in the following ways.

- It can *legitimize grief* and *different styles of grieving*.
- It can provide *structure and stability* during chaos and instability.
- It can *raise self-esteem*, as participating in the ritual shows us as positively impacting on the world.
- Being time-limited, it can offer *safety*, allowing expression of emotion.
- It is a *potent honoring* of a person, relationship, or issue.
- It can *clarify issues* and *encourage changes* in attitudes and behaviors.
- A sense of *direction or meaning* in life can emerge.
- At a time when we feel disconnected or different from others, it can give us a *sense of community* as others support and witness our process.

- It *promotes congruency* (body, mind, emotions, spirit working together).
- It provides *motivation for growth* as participants make public statements of intent to change.

Great stuff! But only if there are helpful elements in the ritual. Good intentions alone do not make a good ritual, as Reverend Bob discovered. Reverend Peter was in great demand for funerals. His services touched people deeply and, at times, increased subsequent church attendance. Bob attended one of Peter's funerals, since he realized his own lacked power. The ritual moved him and he left with the impression of masses of flowers and a few hymns that brought tears to his eyes. And he hadn't even known the deceased!

For his next funeral, Bob eagerly implemented these new ingredients. The immediate family was somewhat sticky about the flowers; it seems Mary had requested no arrangements. Bob provided some himself and the church looked like a garden. The service was a powerful one for Bob, and he noticed that Mary's daughter Deborah went through numerous tissues.

Bob's satisfaction was blunted as the mourners filed out of the church. One elderly woman complained to another, "A bit of a slap in the face to Mary's memory, having all those blooms about. With her being so allergic, her own funeral woulda killed her if she hadn't been dead already." The other replied, "Poor Debby has hay fever as bad as her mom. Did you see the problem she was having breathing during the service?" The "helping hand" strikes again!

In my study, I found the following elements need to be present for a ritual to be effective.

- The goal for the ritual, and/or the issue it is being developed to address, needs to be clarified.
- It needs to be personalized. Symbols important to the grievers make the ritual more meaningful. Some choose a ritual from a cultural tradition different from their own, for example, Native or Celtic spirituality, because it seems interesting. It may be more potent and a

closer "fit" to who we are if we look through our own cultural history for rituals. We may be surprised at what we find. We then have a wider choice of elements from our own and other traditions.

- Participation is important. Commitment is needed to get the most out of any experience. Participation is the deepest level of commitment because we give our whole selves. This does not necessarily mean making a speech. Wearing special clothing or just being "present" during the ritual, rather than thinking about what to make for dinner, are ways to participate.
- Take into account the type of ritual it needs to be: preliminal, liminal, or postliminal. If the grievers are still reeling from a sudden loss (liminal stage) and the facilitator of the ritual talks a lot about postliminal issues, for example, "We can let go of our grief now because she is with God," the grievers will feel violated, not understood, and maybe guilty for hurting so much.
- The preparation must be careful. Taking time and putting energy into planning the ritual can be therapeutic in itself.
- Elements of time – past, present, and future – provide a sense of continuity and optimism.

The following are some frequently asked questions.

If I can't attend the ritual, will I always feel unfinished?

Financial difficulties, illness, work or family commitments, or incarceration are a few of the reasons you may be unable to attend a ritual. If it feels important for you to take part in some way, either develop your own ritual, at a convenient time and place, or do what Sandy did. The priest, in England, stated at the start of the service, "This is an international event. Sandy, in North America, is duplicating this service in her own church as I speak."

Another example: As young parents, Dal and Marte were told not to have a funeral for their stillborn son. Nine years later, they honored him and their brief relationship with him by planting a tree.

Should children attend rituals?

Children can receive the same benefits that adults derive from rituals, if they want to be present and if the adults want their presence. Preparation is necessary, however. Explaining the ceremony, letting them check out the setting prior to the ritual, having an adult they trust be with them to answer questions and take them out if necessary, will help young ones feel more comfortable. Sometimes children benefit more from a private ritual that they help create.

Six-year-old Tim felt shy at the goodbye party. He enjoyed, though, photos taken of him in every room of the home he was leaving.

Repeating rituals – is more better?

During the grieving process, a new meaning or situation may call for a ritual. It is not possible to meet all needs in one ceremony. Other rituals may be helpful as time goes by. Many people find that a subsequent ritual needs to be different from the first or the potency is diminished.

Aunty wants a traditional funeral for Uncle, and Sue wants a ceremony at his favorite beach. How can this be resolved?

People can become very emotional about the "correct way" to conduct a ritual, because it is so powerfully meaningful. A discussion, perhaps with a trusted person as mediator, may help. Everyone needs an opportunity to state their goal for the ritual, what symbols will be meaningful, etc. Clarifying these issues often brings family members closer together as they become more respectful of each other's feelings and ideas. The checklist in the "Rituals" journaling section may be useful for each member to complete. More than one rite is always possible and, in fact, may be better than one that has so many elements it becomes overwhelming.

Does a ritual have to be religious?

No. And yet it often is. The ritual usually incorporates our beliefs or philosophy of life as we draw on them to make sense of our loss and grief. If you do not have a conscious belief system, you may get more benefit from the ritual by clarifying your personal philosophy and including it consciously in your ritual. If you don't do this, your beliefs will be reflected anyway in the elements you choose. Consciously examined beliefs can support us more effectively.

Anticipatory Grief – Not!

Anticipatory grief is an unfortunate term. It has generally come to mean "grieving for a loss which has not yet occurred." In my experience, grieving what may or may not happen is only one of many distressing implications experienced prior to an anticipated loss.

Beth, sitting beside the bed of a wasted, terminally ill man lying in a coma, is grieving actual, present losses that are likely impacting on her more intensely than the awareness of her husband's future death. Finding herself essentially a single parent, with financial concerns, and no sexual or other intimate contact with her life partner, fills her with grief. She needs to see these concerns as legitimate and worthy of support.

Many people say, "I can't grieve now, 'it' hasn't happened yet," or "I don't want to give up or even influence the anticipated loss through defeatist thinking." It is helpful, however, to make some plans and decisions about anticipated losses, for example, by writing a will, by searching out support groups for children encountering parental separation or divorce, or by taking a workshop about planning for retirement. Once the planning is complete, fretting about the future just increases anxiety and dissatisfaction with the present.

Grieving current, actual implications will allow you to clarify and meet immediate needs. As well as making the present more livable, it will also raise trust in your ability to deal with loss, encouraging hope for whatever the future brings.

It is interesting where the term "anticipatory grief" first appeared in the professional literature. In 1944, E. L. Lindemann published an article entitled "Symptomatology and Management of Acute Grief." He described wives who had great difficulty living with the uncertainty of their soldier husbands' absence. It was easier for them to believe their husbands had died and they grieved openly. When the men returned, the wives had great difficulty re-establishing the relationship. Lindemann saw this phenomenon as an unhealthy attempt to protect against "what ifs."

During your adjustment to loss, you may find yourself grieving for an anticipated event. You may choose to talk about this as anticipatory grief. If someone tries to label all your grieving as anticipatory, let them know that you are feeling pain about many actual current changes. The other person will then offer you support now, without waiting until the anticipated event has occurred.

Self-Care

Nearly everyone agrees with the statement, "It is important to care for ourselves." And yet we often put our own needs at the bottom of our "To Do List" and then never get to them. Professional helpers are often among the worst for doing this. In workshops, I help people clarify their beliefs about self-care and then work with them to find a number of strategies that will be effective for them.

Here are the beliefs I hold.

- We are social animals and are not meant to live totally independently. Even hermits living in caves tend to have periodic contact with others, if only to purchase supplies they can't provide for themselves. Therefore, reaching out to others for support is not a sign of weakness. Rather, it is a statement of commitment to relationships as vehicles for healing and growth.
- At first in the grieving process, we may be devastated and need massive amounts of help. When possible, though, we need to take responsibility for self-care. No one else should be in the position of continually rescuing us. Asking for what we need is self-care, as is meeting some needs ourselves.

- Finding a variety of self-care strategies will make healing and/or growth more effective. No single strategy will be helpful in every situation.
- A well-used strategy may "wear out" in time. One of my favorite techniques is to sink into a warm, fragrant bubble bath. I realized it was losing its potency one evening when I was worrying about a situation at work and went into the bathroom to start the water. The tub and towels were damp and I realized I had already bathed. Worrying had consumed all my attention and the bath had been taken on "automatic pilot." I was clean, but still burdened. Developing a variety of self-care strategies strengthens our chances of having a "well-fitting" one for each need.

Developing strategies

In a workshop a few years ago, one participant stated she had a wide variety of self-care tools. With a big smile on her face she listed them: chocolate chip cookies, peanut butter cookies, shortbread cookies, sugar cookies. It is so easy to get into a rut around self-care and have all our aids in one category. If you have no strategies for one of the following areas, ask others what they do.

- **Physical** – When you feel disconnected from your body or when it feels stiff, weak, or in pain, something physical is needed. These strategies could include jogging, yoga, or some other form of exercise; massage, reiki, therapeutic touch or another type of body work; bubble baths, snuggling in bed with a hot water bottle or intimate partner, lighting an aromatherapy candle, or eating comfort food.
- **Mental** – When your thoughts are spinning in circles or you want to think about something other than loss, the following may help: crossword or jigsaw puzzles, television, books, movies, attending a lecture, or doing a craft.
- **Emotional** – When your heart feels broken, your emotions raw, you need help for your feelings. Talking to a trusted friend, journaling, listening to calming or stimulating music, walking in the woods are all ways that can nurture us emotionally.

- **Spiritual** – When faith is shaken, when you feel disconnected from the Source of being, when you want to throw yourself into the love and peace of the divine, when questions about the meaning of life disturb, sustenance for your spirit is needed. Prayer, meditation, soul supporting music, attending religious or healing services or reading inspirational books may provide this.

Most strategies will overlap categories. To find the most effective strategy at any one time, open to your pain and ask yourself what you need to ease it. The message may come immediately or after a few minutes, so try to be patient. You can trust yourself to clarify your needs. Sometimes you may begin one strategy and then find another attracts your attention. This is quite common. As one need or aspect of a need is met, other needs surface. So flexibility will help.

It is also valuable to have strategies that we can use daily, strategies that are more potent because they take more time, energy, or money for periodic use; and strategies for times of overwhelming stress or pain. The journal section "Self-Care" gives you space to record a number of strategies.

Specific Self-Care Strategies

The following strategies have been found by many to structure and ease the grieving process. Each one has a journal section in the back of the book.

Symbols

A symbol is an object, word, place, vision, or dream that stands for a meaning other than its obvious or usual one. The symbol can be widely recognized, such as a dove for peace, or personal, such as a song representing your first love. In the book *Man and His Symbols*, the psychotherapist Carl Jung says that the symbol's purpose is to take us out of our ordinary experience. "As the mind explores the symbol it is led to ideas that lie beyond the grasp of reason."

Anne came to me struggling to accept the implications of a car accident that left her body and brain damaged. After four years, she realized that the cognitive deficits, such as difficulty finding the word she wanted, poor memory, crippling fatigue, and inability to process information quickly, would continue – a drastic change from the old Anne, always on the go with a high-powered career.

As she grieved, Anne realized the need to focus more frequently on her present positive qualities and to stop longing for the past; yet she kept forgetting to do so. I suggested she create a symbol for herself. Anne drew her spirit as a warm, glowing, potent sun, able to shine even in the box of her limitations.

When Anne denied her deficits and continually pushed past her limits, she was so exhausted that she could not connect with her spirit and thought it had died. She told me, "The symbol was an absolute turning point. It drew my attention to my spirit and reminds me to stop and focus so I can hold on to her. I carry a card with my symbol in my purse and have some cards in different rooms in my house." Being visual made it more real for Anne.

You may find that drawing some of the following is helpful: your goal, faith, spirit, path, a block or problem, healing, growth.

Affirmations

By tuning in to your thoughts, you may find that you are giving yourself positive or negative messages. This self-talk is a frequent mental activity. A message such as, "You are getting through this pain well," may be heard consciously, or may stay in the unconscious and reach awareness as a wave of satisfaction. Positive self-talk can be supportive and healing during your journey through loss. Negative self-talk can slow or sabotage the adjustment process. Notice your self-talk to see if it is helping or hindering your healing process. If you are frequently undermined by negative self-talk, it may be helpful to seek counseling to learn techniques that will change this pattern.

Since we come to believe what we say, choosing and using positive self-talk over time will change our attitudes and behaviors for the better.

Positive affirmations are a particularly useful type of self-talk since they are easy to remember, concise, and touch us on many levels at once.

Some people like to create affirmations for specific situations, such as the anniversary of the loss. You may want to read your affirmations upon waking each morning and choose an affirmation for the day.

Affirmations can focus on your journey through loss, your faith, philosophy, goals, desires, or just on your attitude to yourself. Examples include, "I am a wonderful creation, capable of healing and growth," or "The grieving process is a healing process." Be very wary of trying to help by giving someone else an affirmation. A statement that I find myself and that feels healing may be experienced by another as a rationalization, a way to minimize or judge their pain.

Dreams

Keeping track of dreams may give information about your needs or the issues that are part of your grieving process. It has been my experience that two dream themes are common during adjustment to loss.

One theme encourages you to face the reality of your loss. For example, you may return to the workplace where you have been laid off or retired from, only to find that the doors are all locked. Or you see your friend who has died, but as you run towards him, he gets farther and farther away.

The other theme reminds you that you will always keep something valuable associated with the missing person, experience, or object within you. So you may dream that you are having a wonderful game of fetch with your beloved dog. Upon waking, you remember that your dog has died. This is not a bad dream, although in the early days of grief you will feel pain. Later, many people are glad to have these reminder dreams and feel happy or warm upon awakening.

If you have had a traumatic experience, such as a car accident or assault, and experience nightmares that increase in frequency, it may be useful to see a helping professional who has experience desensitizing people to intrusive thoughts.

Blocks

We often experience blocks to grief and one of the most common are recurrent, disturbing thoughts that slow rather than help healing. For example, people may fret about the future: "When my adjustment is over, will I be able to get a job (or a relationship)?" I developed the following technique to deal with these disturbing thoughts. Books on assertiveness also cover this issue.

Use as much paper as you need to complete the following questions as fully as possible. Use a separate sheet(s) for each thought you want to stop. Find a container with a lid or closure to keep your work in. A meaningful container can add power to the technique. One woman, wanting to stop fretting about her chronic pain, chose a large empty medication box.

1. Describe the problem or thought you want to stop.
2. Give the problem or thought a short name.
3. How do you feel when you think about it?
4. What have you already done about it?
5. What do you need to do about it now or in the future?
6. When will you look at this writing again?

Whenever a disturbing thought comes, tell it firmly, "This thought is dealt with. Go away!" (or whatever words you like). If a new idea comes, for example, a place to find information, write it on your sheet. At first, take out and read your sheet often. Then your subconscious mind will not fret that you have forgotten the problem. Praise yourself frequently for using this technique. You can also write about thoughts that need thought-stopping in the "Blocks" section (p.137)

Care from Others

I see assistance from others falling into three categories: support, counseling, and psychotherapy. Most people who are grieving simply need support. These grievers may be hurting intensely, but they basically believe they will adjust to the loss without their self-esteem being shredded. At times they may feel pessimistic about seeing the light at the end of the tunnel, although this feeling does not stay long. These people need the following kind of help.

- An ally – at least one person who will be accepting of all feelings and concerns and who shows care and encouragement.
- Information – about community resources, books or pamphlets, counselors, psychotherapists, spiritual directors, support groups, or aids such as large print books, as well as facts about the grieving process, how children grieve, a disease, etc. Grievers usually have little energy to search out information.

If someone in your life wants to be supportive yet is not sure how to go about it, it might be useful to have them read the information in this guide, or at least this section and the "Helping Others" section (p. 73).

A smaller group of grievers will require counseling. They believe the loss or the grieving process is negatively affecting their self-esteem.

Prior to the loss, life seemed good and they saw themselves as quite competent and worthwhile human beings. Now their world is falling apart and a strong, internal message is saying that the grief will not be resolved. Common messages include, "Bad things don't happen to good people," "Strong people don't cry or show deep emotion," "I should accept that this is God's will and not grieve," "Other people have it worse than I do, so I shouldn't be so upset."

The message may have been within us for a very long time without coming to consciousness until the loss occurred, or it may be one we are currently receiving from another person.

Grieving is a natural, healing process, and if a message tells us otherwise, our adjustment will be slowed or halted. It can be extremely difficult, however, to counteract these messages ourselves. A counselor or spiritual director who is trained in the area of loss and grief can help by:

- providing support by being an ally and by giving information;
- providing direction that will clarify the message, by mutually deciding on a modified or new message that will move towards healing

and growth, and by teaching the griever how to implement the change.

Counseling may involve one or a number of sessions.

An even smaller group will find themselves needing psychotherapy. For them, opening to the pain of the loss is "the last straw." Their life history is full of feelings of incompetence, low self-esteem, and unsatisfying relationships. Grievers may finally realize that these stifling patterns are not going to leave on their own. A psychotherapist trained in loss and grief will:

- provide support and direction;
- clarify, explore, and change patterns of attitudes, behaviors, and beliefs that have long been restricting the person.

Psychotherapy is a longer process and people may move in and out of it at various times in their lives as "milestones" occur, such as developing a new relationship.

Tips for receiving help

- **Make your needs known.** Friends and family members can't read your mind. If you are not sure what will be helpful for you, at least tell them what would be *unhelpful*.
- **Use the "grapevine."** In every group to which we belong – family, friends, work, faith community, sports team, etc. – there is at least one person who is excellent at keeping members informed of important news. So contact that person, or have someone else do so.

  The "rumor mill" is probably already operating and group members may be wondering how to help you. Most will be relieved to have direction on the following points: your interest or need to talk about your loss, your desire to be left alone or have company, your food or transportation requirements.
- **When looking for a professional, be an "informed consumer."** Some professionals have wonderful reputations and yet will not be appropriate for you. They may not have specific training or experience with grief and loss. Or you may feel your personalities are

not compatible. Perhaps the therapist has a bubbly manner which is uncomfortable for you, although another person would find that therapist delightful. Entering a therapeutic relationship takes time and energy. You need to feel safe and honored for who you are.

There are many different philosophical schools of thought for counseling and psychotherapy. Ask the therapist to explain how, in their view, the helping process functions, what the goal of counseling is, what their basic assumptions about people are, when and how you will know that this therapy is working.

Ask about the therapist's background, training, and experience. Check which licensing organizations hold them accountable. It is important to know that they belong to a professional group with ethical standards and practices.

- **Do not try to use family or friends as your therapist** (even if they are licensed). Since the therapeutic relationship is entered to change your beliefs, attitudes, and behaviors so you will be able to become more of the person you were meant to be, it is essential that the helper have no vested interest. A loved one always has some idea of how they would like you to change. It is also important, for your self-esteem, that you learn self-care strategies so that you work towards a time to end formal therapy and continue growing on your own.

Often, in a relationship that encourages deep, honest sharing, we feel a joyful communion with the other. You and your therapist may care about each other deeply, but if the relationship moves into a friendship, which means mutual expression and meeting of needs, then therapy will no longer be effective.

Even though a therapeutic relationship may feel equal, it is entered because the helper has specific skills and expertise that the griever agrees to follow. The therapist's words and actions tend to carry more weight. Frustrated family members often say to me, "I told her the exact same thing, but she wouldn't try it until it came from you!"

Sexual intimacy is never a valid part of the therapy process. There are so many issues and expectations around sexuality it is essential that two people considering sexual contact are fully free to consent or not.

- **Sometimes the issue or message that needs to be explored centers around faith or life philosophy.** It may be most appropriate to find a spiritual director. This type of help is generally not well-known. There are people who have received training and supervision in how to help others explore their beliefs. An effective spiritual director will not have a list of "shoulds" for you and may not even be of your faith. They will help you clarify and learn to live the spirituality that is right for you.

  If you are connected to a faith community, it might seem convenient to ask your religious leader to give you spiritual direction. This person may offer you wonderful, much-needed support. The constraints of the effective therapeutic relationship still hold, however. You need someone you will be able to "fire" when you have dealt with your issues.

- **Some people find it extremely difficult or impossible to enter therapy.** They may have financial restrictions, there may be no therapists in their geographical area, etc. With creativity, it is still possible to "do therapy."

  I have had people come for a week and see me every day or every other day. Then we have telephone or letter contact, while they continue to read books relevant to their issue, and journal intensively. Others attend a series of workshops or retreats, or choose a number of books for "bibliotherapy." It is often amazing to realize how many opportunities we see to work on an issue, once we become aware of it.

- **Self-help groups can provide a wonderful feeling of not being alone.** Others who have experienced the same type of loss may help you trust that you too will heal. We are not exactly the same, however. Even if someone else has had a similar experience, they may not have the same needs, or issues. Don't feel you have to follow another's advice because "they've been there."

Complicated Grief

Grief is complicated when it continues to be the center of a person's life for a very long time, and/or when it is extremely intense, and/or when it is incredibly complex.

For some, complicated grief becomes maladaptive, negatively impacting on their self-esteem. Without treatment, it may last their whole lives. For others, complicated grief may be adaptive; the person's self-esteem remains intact. The griever will require more support from others, however, since the process is so exhausting and demanding.

Complicated grief has one or more of the following characteristics.

- The loss was *traumatic*, being an experience of intense fear, horror, or helplessness.
- The *personal meaning* of the loss seems impossible to resolve. It may involve strong guilt, loss of faith, hopelessness, or helplessness.
- A *pre-existing pattern*, such as depression or anxiety, means the griever has fewer emotional, physical, spiritual, or mental resources to draw on to deal with the current loss.
- An *accumulation of loss* makes this one "the last straw."
- The *wrong type* or *absence of support* leaves the griever feeling judged and alone.

If complicated grief becomes maladaptive, we may experience a clinical depression, anxiety or adjustment disorder, or repress the effects or reality of the loss to such an extent that it is no longer thought about or, for some, even remembered. All these reactions that hinder a person's healing are treatable.

Symptoms of maladaptive grief may include adaptive ones that are more intense or do not diminish. Common symptoms are frequent nightmares, a desire or attempt to hurt or kill one's self or another, intense guilt, hate, reliving the traumatic experience, strong anxiety when thinking or talking about the loss, becoming anxious about anything that reminds you of the loss, feeling strongly disconnected from yourself or others, intense apathy or depression, and feeling strong helplessness or hopelessness.

Expensive emotions

I define "expensive emotions" as those that cost a great deal in energy and time. Furthermore, they are life-denying, keeping us from healing and growth. Common expensive emotions include bitterness, envy, jealousy, shame, resentment, vengeance, guilt, despair, and powerlessness.

Some grievers believe they need these emotions to keep from total collapse, or to give them the motivation to work for change of laws or services, such as an overpass on a busy street where their child was killed. In the section on forgiveness, we explored how expensive emotions like bitterness or resentment can give the illusion of power, while pushing the griever to violence of thought, word, or action.

Expensive emotions encourage grievers to view the world with a very intense, narrow focus. Grievers and their cause/concern lose credibility and other people withdraw support. Those who believe expensive emotions are protective use so much energy in these defenses that there is little or none for life enhancement.

An expensive emotion can be transformed by, first, realizing how restrictive it is and then by looking for a life-affirming emotion to put in its place. For example, I might substitute determination to enhance children's safety for bitterness and resentment at the municipal authorities who had not provided an overpass.

Consciously encouraging this determination and "thought-stopping" every time I experience the bitterness and resentment, will help the shift. Expensive emotions that are very strong and that have lived with us for a long time may need stronger "medicine" in the form of individual or group counseling or psychotherapy.

Helping Others

Often, we do not grieve alone. Family members, friends, and, at times, whole communities and nations may also be in mourning. If you want to help others while you are grieving, a few points will allow you to be more effective.

- **Meet your own needs in grief.** This can actually be extremely helpful for other grievers. When we let others help us, we act as a good role model, which will make it more likely that others will honor their own grief. One six-year-old, whose father had abandoned the family, told me emphatically, "I'm not gonna be a mommy when I grow up. If anything bad happens, you have to spend all your time looking after the kids. You don't get to have any fun." Her mother was worn to the bone, believing that to be a good single parent, she had to meet all of her children's needs herself.

  Also, knowing we are looking after ourselves will calm the worry our loved ones have about us, allowing them to get on with their own adjustment.

- **Allow others to grieve.** It is natural to want to shield those we love from pain, and yet loss is a natural part of life. Hiding our own fears and concerns slows our own adjustment and often results in others feeling disconnected from us, and, therefore, more concerned about us. Trying to stop another's pain gives the message that their feelings are wrong. They may then try to hide their feelings from you.

  Allowing others to meet their needs in the way that helps them most can be a real gift. In one family session, Pam told me that she worried because her older son, Jason, had not talked to her about his brother's upsetting diagnosis. Jason squirmed and looked at the floor. I replied that Jason would know what help he required. The boy looked up and said, "I would like to talk to my friends, but I don't because I know it would hurt Mom if she knew I was talking to them instead of her." Pam was able to assure him that she would be relieved to know that he was getting the kind of help he really wanted.

- **Let the children and adults around you have the gift of caring for you.** Although you don't want others to feel they have to help, it can feel extremely satisfying to give to another.

  One teen, who had attended a talk I gave at his school after a ski bus accident, said, "I went home that night and my dad snapped at us at the dinner table. I told him that a lady at school gave us a list of normal symptoms of grief, and that irritability towards those you love is a big one. Dad actually said thank you, he hadn't known that and was feeling guilty about his snapping. I think that's the first time I've been able to teach my dad something."

- **Check out by asking.** Rather than make assumptions about what is needed, ask what would be helpful. One new widow came to see me after Christmas and complained, "When I arrived home the other day, there were five turkey casseroles on my doorstep. I don't like turkey! Now I have to decide what to do with them instead of being able to stay with my feelings about Nathan. Also, I have five friends who feel they have helped me and they haven't. What do I say to them? Why couldn't they have just asked if I wanted the casserole?"

  Even if someone does not know what they want, they may be able to tell you what they don't want. Needs can change very quickly, so check out often. Giving your own motivation for helping can show the other that you do not see them as weak. I suggest something like, "I would like to do something to show my caring for you, but I don't know what would be helpful." If you have suggestions, give a number of them so your loved one won't feel that you need to help in a certain way.

- **Check out by acting.** Sometimes it feels inappropriate to ask if a type of help would be acceptable. In that case, carefully watching the other's verbal and body response as you offer the help in a tentative and gentle manner will give you the information you need. For example, I may think my friend is feeling guilty. So I say, "I was reading something about grief that said it is normal to experience guilt after a loss." My friend is then free to drop or continue the topic. Questions demand; statements invite.

This strategy can also be useful when deciding whether to hug or hold a friend. A hug, if wanted, can help more than a thousand words. Given at the wrong time, it feels extremely intrusive. If I think a friend wants a hug, and yet I'm not certain, I reach out and touch him on his shoulder or hand, and immediately withdraw. If the touch was welcome and he wants more, he will move towards me in some manner – leaning forward, or putting out his hands. If he does not want further touch, he may move his body away from me slightly.

- **Listen.** Being able to express feelings and concerns to a caring, accepting friend can be very healing. We have a tendency to offer advice in an attempt to speed the other's healing, or to save them from mistakes we have made. Advice usually feels disrespectful and the griever wonders if you are really hearing them or are willing to be with them in their pain. If your friend asks about your experience, tell them briefly, and add that you know that there are many ways to feel or deal with such a situation. Silent, interested, non-judgmental listening can be deeply healing.

- **Offer information.** Grieving people often have a difficult time searching out resources to help them. Offering your knowledge about a book you found useful, or an agency that provides support for this type of loss, may be very welcome. Be sensitive when you offer information and back off if it is met with resistance or disinterest. Pushing information can feel like a judgment to "get over it."

May you move surely towards your goal on the path through loss.

BIBLIOGRAPHY

General grief and loss

Bridges, William. *Transitions: Making Sense of Life's Changes.* Reading, MA: Addison-Wesley Publishing Co., 1980.

Dayton, Tian. *Heartwounds: The Impact of Unresolved Trauma and Grief on Relationships.* Deerfield Beach, FL: Health Communications, Inc., 1997.

Lindemann, E. L. "Symptomatology and Management of Acute Grief." *American Psychiatrist* (1944): 141–149.

Moustakas, Clark E. *Loneliness.* Englewood Cliffs, NJ: Prentice Hall, 1961.

Schneiderman G. *Coping with Death in The Family.* Toronto: Chimo, 1979.

Viorst, Judith. *Necessary Losses:.* New York: Simon & Schuster, 1986.

Wylie, Betty Jane. *New Beginnings: Living through Loss and Grief.* Toronto: Key Porter Books, Ltd., 1991.

Past experiences with loss

Grollman, Earl. *Living When a Loved One Has Died.* Boston: Beacon Press, 1977.

Reeves, Nancy. *Understanding Loss: A Parents' Guide.* Vancouver: British Columbia Council for the Family, 1991. (604) 660-0675 or 1-800-663-5638

Ritual

Driver, Tom. *The Magic of Ritual: Our Need for Liberating Rites that Transform Our Lives and Our Communities.* San Francisco: Harper, 1991.

Turner, Victor. *The Ritual Process: Structure and Anti-structure.* Chicago: Aldine, 1969.

van Gennep, A. *Rites of Passage.* Translated by M. Vizedom and G. Caffee. Chicago: University of Chicago Press, 1960.

Self-care

Bloom, William. *Psychic Protection: Creating Positive Energies for People and Places*. New York: Simon & Schuster, 1996.

Colgrove, M., H. Bloomfield, and P. McWilliams, *How to Survive the Loss of a Love*. New York: Bantam, 1977.

Keleman, Stanley. *Living Your Dying*. New York: Random House, 1974.

Spirituality and philosophy

Campbell, Joseph, and Bill Moyers. *The Power of Myth*. New York: Doubleday, 1988.

Frankl, Victor. *Man's Search for Meaning*. New York: Washington Square Press, 1963.

Jung, C. G., ed. *Man and His Symbols*. London: Aldus Books, 1964.

Kushner, Harold. *When Bad Things Happen to Good People*. New York: Avon Books, 1981.

Lewis, C. S. *A Grief Observed*. New York: Seabury Press, 1963.

Peck, M. Scott. *People of the Lie: The Hope for Healing Human Evil*. New York: Simon & Schuster, 1983.

Popov, Linda Kavelin, Dan Popov, and John Kavelin. *The Family Virtues Guide: Simple Ways to Bring the Best Out of Our Children and Ourselves*. New York: Plume Books, 1997.

Rupp, Joyce. *Praying Our Goodbyes*. Notre Dame: Ave Maria Press, 1988.

Savary, Louis and Patricia Berne. *Kything: The Art of Spiritual Presence*. Mahwah, NJ: Paulist Press, 1988.

Soelle, Dorothee. *Suffering*. Philadelphia: Fortress Press, 1975.

Other publications by Nancy Reeves

Reeves, Nancy. *Understanding Loss: A Parents' Guide*. Vancouver: British Columbia Council for the Family, 1991. (604) 660-0675 or 1-800-663-5638

—. "Ritual As Therapeutic Intervention for Maladaptive Grief: A Phenomenological Mapping." Ph.D. diss., University of Alberta, 1989.

PART FOUR

JOURNAL
SECTIONS

HOW AM I TODAY?

How Am I Today?

This is the place for free writing about your experiences, feelings, and concerns. Dating each entry makes it more interesting when you re-read it. Mention material that you are writing in another section such as "Dreams" or "New Awareness."

GRIEF EXPERIENCE CHECKLIST

GRIEF EXPERIENCE CHECKLIST

Being immersed in an emotion, it is easy to believe we will stay there forever. This checklist allows you to see the ebb and flow of your feelings. It is natural to experience one emotion strongly for a time, then find it barely there, only to have it resurface later, stronger than ever. If a feeling seems to be "stuck" at an intense level for an extended period, counseling may be helpful.

*Pick a number from 1-10 (1=barely present, 10=overwhelming)

DATE	Sadness	Anger	Loneliness	Relief	Anxiety	Hopelessness	Love	Peace	Happiness	Frustration	Depression	Notes

DATE	Sadness	Anger	Loneliness	Relief	Anxiety	Hopelessness	Love	Peace	Happiness	Frustration	Depression	Notes

DATE	Sadness	Anger	Loneliness	Relief	Anxiety	Hopelessness	Love	Peace	Happiness	Frustration	Depression	Notes

DATE	Sadness	Anger	Loneliness	Relief	Anxiety	Hopelessness	Love	Peace	Happiness	Frustration	Depression	Notes

ENERGY MOVEMENT

ENERGY MOVEMENT

Read the section "Energy Management" and then complete an energy circle. Think about your activities for the past few days and decide the percentage of energy that you are using for survival, grieving/readjustment, and life enhancement. Complete another circle whenever you wish. Most people find weekly at the beginning and later, every two or three weeks, is most useful.

Remember, an act could look like one type of energy and really be another. For example, I may think I have life enhancement energy since I went to a movie. But if my motive for going was to have two hours escape from thinking of my loss, that would fit better within grieving as a self-care strategy.

DATE: _____

DATE: _____

DATE: _____

DATE: _____

DATE: _____

DATE: _____

NEW AWARENESS

NEW AWARENESS

At times, you will encounter an awareness about yourself, your loss, adjustment process, beliefs, etc. that will enhance your movement to healing or growth. When first brought to awareness, it will seem that the insight is so powerful it will never be forgotten. As time goes by, though, it will fade to the back of your mind. Writing it here will keep it fresh. You may also find it useful to write changes in attitude and/or behavior that you will make, based on the new awareness.

SPIRITUAL ISSUES

SPIRITUAL ISSUES

Record here any struggles, insights, and questions that relate to your beliefs. Remember, any feeling or thought is acceptable. If necessary, re-read "Spirituality" (p. 43).

AFFIRMATIONS

AFFIRMATIONS

When you find or create an affirmation that nourishes you, write it here.

BLOCKS

BLOCKS

When you discover a block or restriction to your adjustment, write it here rather than in "How Am I Doing Today?" so it won't get lost. You can also add more entries as you work through the block either alone or with the help of a friend or professional.

An example of a common block is being very good at giving support but not being able to accept support from others. You become aware of how this pattern is slowing your healing. This knowledge is a wonderful and necessary first step to resolving the block. To benefit from this awareness you will need to let others help you. This is probably easier said than done. You may need to explore many aspects of this issue including what beliefs you have held that make asking for support so difficult. It takes time and energy to work through blocks such as this one, yet the result can be freeing.

SYMBOLS

SYMBOLS

Draw symbols here to give yourself encouragement and hope as you move through the grieving process. Your initial symbol may transform over time as your personal needs change. For example, Brenda and Dano both saw themselves as fragile insects being buffeted and threatened by their loss. As her needs became clearer, Brenda realized she needed to accept the grieving process, be gentler on herself, and allow more rest and renewal time. She then drew herself as a caterpillar entering a cocoon, knowing that she would eventually emerge as a butterfly. Dano was struck by how isolated his insect looked. He knew he had been pushing his friends away who were offering support. Thinking about this, he remembered the instruction he was given in childhood: "Be a man and do it on your own." He saw how this message was restricting him and drew himself as a bee living in the supportive community of a large hive.

DREAMS

DREAMS

In this section, record your dreams. There are many ways to explore the feeling or content of dreams. Your local library or bookstore will have some good instructional books.

RITUALS

RITUALS

Read the section "Ritual" for information on the benefits of ritual. Use this section to record ceremonies that you have developed or participated in during your healing process. If you wish to create a ritual, answering the following questions will provide an initial structure for you. Transfer the questions to another sheet to give yourself as much space as needed for your answers.

1. What is the purpose of this ritual?

2. What elements would you like to include from previous rituals?

3. As you think about the purpose of this ritual, what would be meaningful to include? music – symbolic objects – colors – activities – readings

4. Whom would you like to attend?

5. What would you like others to do?

6. What would you like to do yourself?

7. Where do you want it to be held?

8. How long do you want it to last?

9. When do you want it to take place?

10. How do you want to announce it?

11. Who do you want to help you organize your wishes and choreograph this ritual?

SELF-CARE

SELF-CARE

Read the information sections "Self-Care" and "Care from Others." As you become aware of activities that lower your stress level, write them down. It is often difficult to remember self-care strategies when feeling intense emotional, physical, or spiritual pain. If others suggest interesting strategies to you, write them initially under new strategies until you can test them.

Try to include physical, emotional, mental, and spiritual strategies in each section.

Daily self-care strategies

(Examples: talking to a loved one, warm bath, meditation or prayer, playing or listening to music.)

Daily self-care strategies, continued

Periodic self-care strategies

(Examples: dinner or movie, night or weekend away, a nurturing work-shop or retreat, counseling, buying something special.)

During verwhelming stress

(Examples: allowing family/friends to pick up your survival functions, more intense counseling, longer holiday or retreat.)